For my dad
instilling a love of his..y,
into my life and making it fun
and enjoyable

For my mom
positively nurturing my
creativity and allowing it
to blossom

This is a work of creative nonfiction. Some parts
have been fictionalized in varying degrees, for various purposes.

Written by Aaron Mathieu

ISBN: 9798664292534

It was in a small town
Named Churubusco

Welcome to Churubusco

Something BIG happened
So long ago

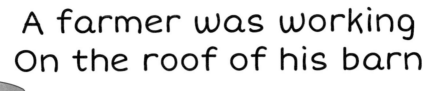

A farmer was working
On the roof of his barn

As the sun shined down
All across his farm

4

He sat for a moment
Beneath the warm sky

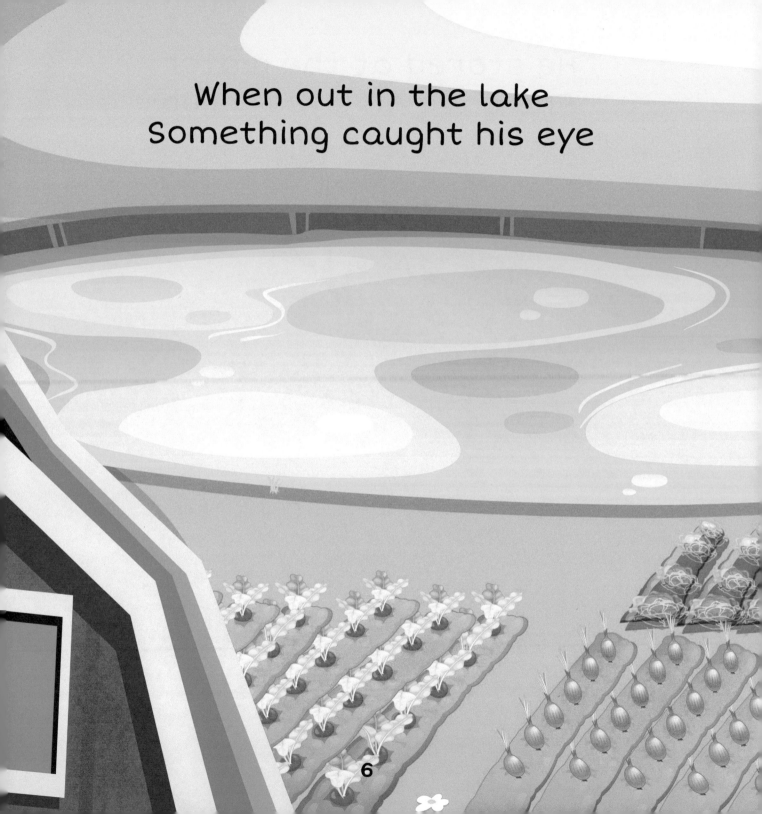

When out in the lake
Something caught his eye

He stared at the water
And gave his eyes a rub

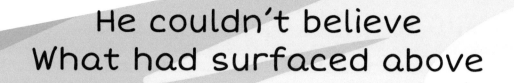

He couldn't believe
What had surfaced above

His mouth opened wide
He never saw such a sight

A huge turtle they called "Oscar"
Basked in the sunlight

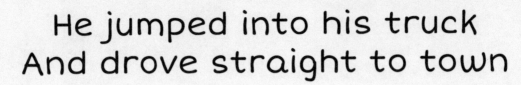

He jumped into his truck
And drove straight to town

To tell all of his friends
About the turtle he'd found

His friends they all laughed
Nobody believed him

So he drove back home
And said, "I'll prove to them"

He made some traps
And a very large net

"I'll catch this turtle
I'll catch him yet!"

Oscar hid in the water
Deep down below

The tired old farmer
Searched to and fro

He tried pumping the water
All out of the lake

It plugged up the tractor
Oh what a mistake!

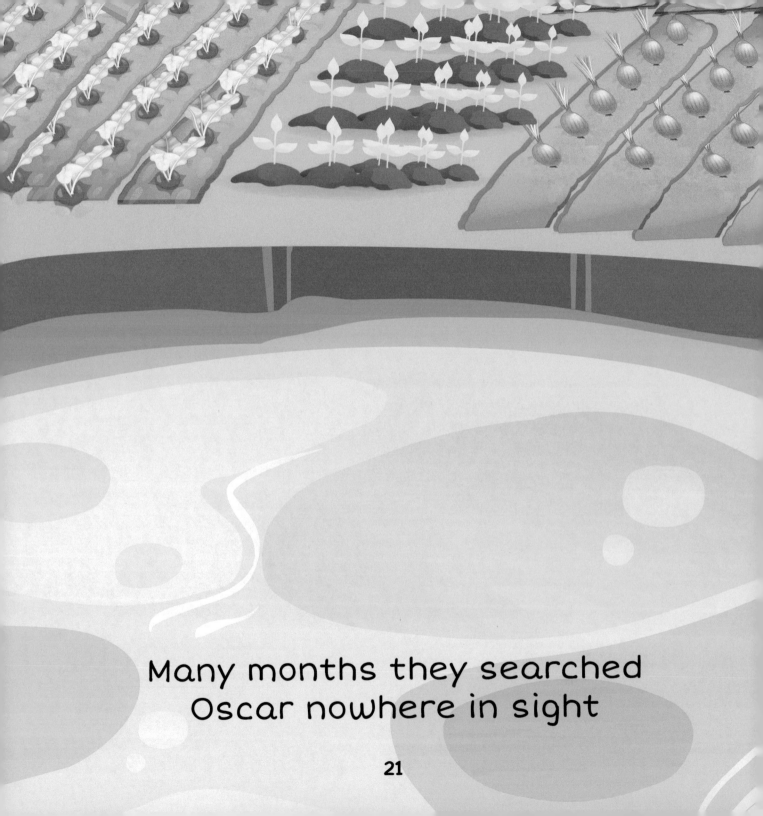

Many months they searched
Oscar nowhere in sight

Where is Oscar?
Where did he go?

Is he still out there?
Nobody knows.

Made in the USA
Columbia, SC
23 March 2024

33523741R00015